Pg 38 - Beth
40
Pg 68 - Judge
pg 47 - Consci.

Pg 60,
Pg 71

good - earlier
Excellent
a.m.y 6/28/88

Awakening from
the Dream of Me

Awakening from the Dream of Me

by David Manners

Non-Stop Books ✆ Minneapolis

Published by Non-Stop Books
P.O. Box 24732
Minneapolis, Minnesota 55416

Grateful acknowledgment is made to Seed Center for permission to reprint selected passages from *Look Through*, by David Manners, copyright © 1971 by David Manners.

Library of Congress Cataloging in Publication Data

Manners, David 1900–
Awakening from the dream of me.

Bibliography: p.
1. Spiritual life.   2. Consciousness.   I. Title.
BL624.M343 1987   126   86-83358
ISBN 0-936816-10-4

Oh man with sightless eyes and empty heart
awaken from the dream of me
and see the wondrous I thou art.

Contents

Acknowledgments

Without the love and encouragement of dear friends, books large or small on this subject would not appear. Thus, I especially wish to thank William and Rachel Samuel, John Bailey, and many others united in the wonder of this conscious awareness we are.

Introduction

There is a divine kernel deep within each of us which, when it begins to blossom, brings an awakening sense of wonder and delight. That Entity within, splendidly bright, defies a direct look with ordinary eyes. Like the sun, it goes down in the evening and rises in the morning. Behind and beyond the words that tell of it is an enthusiasm of spirit, a childlikeness that marvels at the wonder of life. That divine imprint within tells us of Awareness being aware, of Awareness' new world.

David Manners is one who marvels at the wonder of life. I remember many years ago, under the great redwoods of Big Sur, a group of us watched as he knelt by a stream, took a bright stone from the ancient gravel, and saw it with new eyes. David speaks of that time much as I tell of a pond where everything became new to me in the twinkling of an eye. Since those days under the red-woods, we have watched David live Awareness as Identity ever more fully. We have seen him shed his earlier sense of things, just as a cicada sheds its shell, a butterfly its cocoon.

Awakening from the Dream of Me describes part of David's journey. It is one of those shouts of joy we are all one day destined to make. This book tells of the wonder of looking within and finding God's child unfettered and free, still very much alive, untouched by the tribulations of time.

William Samuel

Awakening from the Dream of Me

CHAPTER ONE

Awakening

Awakening

The galaxies, suns, and planets am I,
the simplest weed or blade of grass,
the cricket piping on the hearth,
all these and more am I.

We dream away our lives wrapped in cocoons, patterning our lives on the past, repeating old errors. Only when we awaken from the mortal dream do we discover the reality of our being.

When we have been freed of all concepts of God, Jesus, and Buddha and we stand naked with nothing to cling to, then are we open and vulnerable, ready to understand. This is when seeing truth is possible.

You never know when the curtain of the me-sense will suddenly rise to reveal the blazing light of reality. It does not occur, however, as a result of convenience, meditation, or prayer.

❧

Some come into the light of full seeing instantly. Others take years of time on earth to surrender the me-sense.

❧

Now I am free, alive, and awake! I listen for the voice of the Self and find it everywhere—in the twittering of robins, the squawk of a jay. I see its reflection in the face of a young child, in the petal of a roadside flower, and in the silence of trees in the forest.

Love, which expands my heart to include the universe, tells me of infinite wonders yet to know.

❧

You already are your perfect Self. It's only a matter of recognition. There never was, is, or will be more perfection than you are at this perfect moment.

❧

If I could tell you, really tell you, of the revelation available to us here and now, it might instantly burn off the person-mask and all its armor. But I can't even put it into words for myself, for words are too limiting. I can, however, furnish a clue to the vastness of the infinite wonder we call "isness."

The question, "What do I do about Self-realization?" presupposes there is *someone* to do something about it. This question comes from a sense of duality, which in itself makes any answer incongruous.

Why, I am the son of that which is. I am no slave of sickness, struggle, and death. I am heir to the kingdom given me, that now I claim as mine. I am my master and my government. I am infinite and eternal life. Awareness is what I am, all I am.

Suddenly I am immersed in a boundless void with no top, no bottom, no start, no finish, no time—no measurement of any kind. There is no darkness, no light, not a particle of anything known. Yet it is more familiar than my own breath.

I am reborn. All is made new to me upon awakening. I am no longer a creature of human limitations. I am aware.

There is nothing to achieve or acquire within this serenity. I see an unlimited, open universe.

When awakening is no longer a word, concept, or desire, it becomes a fact. Then will I move with my being as consciousness. Then am I awareness itself!

There is no route nor goal. So give up reading the works of enlightened ones in hope of achievement. There is nothing to achieve.

It's up to us to decide whom we serve. For once we *know* we are not separate from the universe, we no longer need teachers.

When we discover the truth in the heart of the Self where it has always been, we can then free ourselves from the books and papers.

The common belief about liberation is that it is something difficult to attain. But it's so utterly simple and happy beyond happiness, free beyond freedom, powerful beyond power. It's the wonder of wonders, the very I, I am.

Not until I knew the wind as I — rather than as a force out there in the canyon battering at my window — was my seeing, feeling, and hearing of the wind transformed into serenity. Here, closer than the pillow that my head lies on, the wild wind lulls me to sleep.

Is this so difficult to see, feel, and know? No. Seeing consciousness or God as everything is gloriously simple.

Before awakening, you must give up everything. You let go and plunge alone into the void where there is no book or gentle voice to cling to. From then on, words are useless. Being and evidencing take the place of teachings.

Through relinquishing old concepts, we finally come to the real and eternal Self.

✻

I am no longer bound by my conception of self as a worthless, separate sinner. Nor am I bound by beliefs which need political leaders, doctors, teachers, priests, or gurus. Do you know this freedom?

✻

While it's easy to say, "I am unbound," can we really be unbound without feeling the presence of God? Without knowing this in the heart, there can be no seeing. It cannot be talked about; it must be lived.

✻

Freed from the slavery of concepts, opinions, and ego-darkness, I awaken from my dream life and embrace the reality I am.

✻

What is there to do about consciousness but *be* it, to know the joy and light of it here and now in the present and eternal moment?

✻

This state of being is one of grace, of readiness to again find the unadulterated little one, the pure child of God. It is a state of openness that cannot be reconciled with anything that occurred before.

In Self-realization there is nothing to gain. You simply recognize who and what you really are—and always have been—apart from that false appearance of a so-called born human being.

Awakening is similar to the phenomenon of experiencing the past and future as ceasing to exist. The wonder of the present moment destroys all belief in space and time, leaving only infinite being.

At first I wanted to measure my progress. I still needed to have someone tell me I was doing well. That need disappeared when I discovered that there is no place to progress toward, nothing to become. All I am is already the entity I am.

Now when I consider *isness*, I begin to understand what it means. It is *nowness*, this moment as I write on paper, this line _____ I draw, this instant of conscious awareness in which I write, act, and live.

Here, in this place, in this eternal moment *I exist*. I am the tangible I see, as well as the intangible I sense.

I am on this planet as it sweeps around the sunstar in one of countless galaxies. I feel the perfection of this moment. I experience the beauty of the universe as a promise of infinite wonders beyond present understanding.

Obj Consc is a part of un. Consc not beyond it.

The Self is consciousness unclouded by human thoughts. When the illusion of personal sense is surrendered, the resplendent Self unfolds. Only then is the dreary wheel of birth and death overcome. We are released into love sublime, the boundlessness of life eternal.

How could I have dreamed for so long—unaware of who and what I am?

Even if we are aware of a Self that is one with consciousness, this does not mean we are liberated. As long as we feel attached to any illusion of the person-self and its lifelong conditioning of the mind with its judgments based on false learning, we are still far from true liberation.

Bliss, as has been said, is a way station, a resting place, and not a goal. Bliss is only another something to hold on to. We let go of thoughts which shuttle themselves back and forth from one subject to another. We watch this process until it stops. Only when thoughts disappear is awareness experienced in all its splendor as the warp and woof of all being.

Oh hear the cry of those awakened
By a clap of thunder
Their laughter shakes the stars.

The sudden revelation is not a thing of time, prayer, meditation, or convenience. It happens when and where it happens, regardless of place or preparation. Even if it has happened several times before, it is always a surprise.

During a struggle to recall a great experience I had once delighted in, I couldn't see that it was closer than my heartbeat. Exhausted and weary, I gave up. I surrendered all effort to *do* anything. Suddenly I realized that the experience was the very *I* I had been seeing — my world, my universe, and beyond.

The divine fool is dedicated to the wonder and glory of conscious awareness. With eyes too pure to behold evil, s/he sees only light, energy, and life in the eternal now. The divine fool knows only consciousness, pure and undefiled as the deity, principle, and Christ. The ultimate message of the divine fool? Simply that God is everything and everything is God and not an iota of anything else.

Liberation comes from knowing that perfection is here and now. Infinity is here and now. Birthless, ageless, deathless, free from clocks and measurements, we *are* this moment forever in the eternal moment.

When this knowing is a daily hour-by-hour, moment-by-moment experience, we are free to be fully open to the omnipresence of consciousness. This is Self-evidence or Self-realization.

O mighty One of love beyond opposites, this I, I am, knows no measure of great and small. I am this blade of grass, this grain of sand, this drop of water, and every atom of this body. I stand in awe of this wonder that I am.

CHAPTER TWO

The Me-Illusion

The Me-Illusion

It's only the belief
in a separate me
that keeps realization at bay.

How easy it is to get involved with the mind and its con-
cern with money, clothes, friends, likes and dislikes! All
these trifles go on while consciousness is present.

We constantly ignore the wonder we are, settling for
dust, rather than the real wealth that is ours.

How long have I been a slave to that limited person who
must possess all he desires? All I own is a skeleton in a
grave, a corpse — nothing more.

No sooner had I begun this path of seeing the truth about myself, than the me-sense or ego began to struggle for its survival. Now I know that all illusions — even the illusion of the me-sense — disappear before the light of truth.

Without an open heart, without giving and receiving love, I live a death far worse than any surrender of that limited person known as David.

If we run our lives according to human will, we miss life's wonder. Most of us live the way we were taught and conditioned. We rely on the me-sense, the me-wants to guide us. We live a difficult life of brief pleasure, grim disappointment, struggle, and tension leading to pain, sickness, and often, disillusionment with living.

Yet all these difficulties have a purpose. Unless we are addicted to misery, we will be drawn in time toward better ways of living. Those of us who have experienced tragedy are usually most ready to relinquish the me-sense.

Only when the me-person is absent can wholeness be realized. Only when there is an absence of wishing, imaging, and analyzing can awakening occur. This is not as difficult as it sounds. Indeed, all that is real is the unencumbered I, the conscious awareness of your existence.

The personal sense knows nothing but its dream. Belief in its existence means slipping into an ever deeper shadow. There truth is all but obscured; but truth is never completely hidden. There is always enough light for us to find our way out of darkness into revealment. For without darkness, there would be no light; darkness delineates light.

Often, after a sound sleep, I awaken to find my mind empty of any thoughts or recollection of my history or sense of having been born. I experience nothing but the light of morning and a deep sense of bliss. Where is the person of worries and responsibilities, of passion and conniving? Gone! There is only bliss and a bird's sweet song.

(Bliss, of course, is a resting place — not a goal. It is like a backwater in the river where, if one isn't alert, one simply twirls, like a leaf separated from the mainstream.)

For some, the experience of forgetting the self is terrifying. Many shake themselves and return to their fears, worries, hopes, and dreams. They look sadly at that fading moment of bliss, seeing the hopelessness of being chained to that limited person they think themselves to be.

Free of the me-sense, I get a glimpse of the enormity of awareness. Dead to the me-person, I am that principle which is life itself.

an Ever-Present Consc,

Let what consciousness is be, for it *will be*, regardless of any possessive *I* that tries to alter it to my personal liking. Struggling against that which is, is foolish. To struggle is to die. To *let be* is to live and awaken.

How many of us dare lay down the burden of the me-sense to enter the infinite wonder where there are no words? How many of us dare to see what the *I* really is?

Consciousness, or what my friend William Samuel calls the "inner child," is always present. When you actually live this presence, you stop questioning it. Then you are one with consciousness and the me-sense seems a laughable mistake.

Regardless of whether it is experienced as horrendous or enchanting, the me-sense exists for a purpose: it teaches us truth.

CHAPTER THREE

The Intellect

The Intellect

What slakes the burning hunger to give,
to express the heartfelt and the known?
Words, the only tool, fail utterly.

Let go of the paraphernalia of a preoccupied mind. Become free! Clean the mind of all its rubbish. Mind is never empty. It overflows with the light of unobjectified love.

The mind is a weaving of ideas based on how we have been conditioned to think, react, and desire. Recognizing that it hides our true identity is the first step in returning to the divine wonder of our existence.

We, on this planet, know nothing. We have forgotten the purity of spirit, the child within us.

The simpler and more childlike our approach, the easier our comprehension of truth.

Children don't write books *about* what makes them laugh, clap, and play. Their joy is unmarred by thinking. They *are* the joy — the clapping, the playing.

Only later do they learn society's do's and don'ts. Often this training to become so-called good citizens kills their natural union with life.

The way to discover the Self is to bypass the programmed mind and begin anew. Let go all judgments and open yourself to the wonder of a heart experiencing the perfection of love.

Many distrust the heart and must have everything proven by logic. Yet logic is not the source of truth. It may help put what comes from the heart on to paper. But as a foundation, the intellect is of little value.

A huge gap exists between intellectually accepting truth and experiencing it. The moment you know truth, a tremendous change and expansion occurs in your understanding of consciousness. No longer is your thinking confined to a space enclosed within the skull.

We cannot use logic to define God. The sooner the reasoning mind makes way for the heart's truth, the sooner we see the simplicity of reality is present in the eternal now. It is never *not* present.

Isn't trying to get into heaven with a preoccupied mind like trying to put the proverbial camel through the eye of the needle?

How exhilarating it is to free yourself from old beliefs, to free your mind of institutions you once bowed to!

Ideas are but a comfort blanket we use to hide from existence, which scares the nonexisting *I* we cling to.

Watch what happens to the mind when it encounters ideas outside its programming. Doesn't it grow weary? Doesn't it resist, rather than consider anything outside its accepted patterns?

No books or gurus can awaken us. They are but signposts. If we study signposts, we only go in the direction pointed to.

    We should not, of course, ignore books, teachers, and gurus; they show us the way. Yet no matter how much we read, meditate, or study with teachers, we ourselves must experience that which is beyond words.

All knowledge is already known by us. Books simply help us recognize what is already ours.

Words never tell the whole story. At best, they suggest the infinitude of being. What I write is but a shadow of the experience.

Dare we relinquish all we have been taught to believe? Dare we cease leaning on that rickety scaffolding that makes up our personal conditioning?

Words cannot tell of the peace and joy beyond understanding. The intuitive heart knows these things. Only the awakened can experience them.

What is the use of knowledge when it's destined to be transcended? Knowledge of the Self is the only knowledge worth knowing. When we know the Self, we know all. The Self is transcendent and eternal. It is consciousness unclouded by human thought.

Words are like bits of paper, dropped at intervals in the trackless forest, to guide the one who cares to use them.

The path to Self-discovery is strewn with those who could not take that last step toward liberation. They know all the words and repeat them until they lose all meaning.

Often, we are tempted to discount our simple under-
standings and go seeking elsewhere, while the ultimate
wisdom is here. The wonder you and I are—*that* is
wisdom.

Though the intellect seems to consist of a series of dis-
tracting thoughts coming from the mind, this is but a
smoke screen that hides the true Self. To rid ourselves of
the smoke screen, we must become still and watch the
mind until it slows down and stops. Then we will experience pure consciousness. This awareness is the
highest wisdom.

Words are not important. It is what appears between
them that sounds the bell and calls the unawakened to
realization.

The limited, so-called thinking mind does not realize its
identity with the Self. It becomes entangled in the illusion that we are separate from God and nature. Then the
wonder of wholeness and oneness escapes us.

No one can learn *for* someone else. No one can teach another. It is only through one's own discovery of the transcendent Self that perfect tranquility is experienced.

We may study ideas, opinions, and experiences, but we always return to the one we are. Consciousness is the teacher and source we rely on. We may read and study for a lifetime, but in the end, we turn to the simplicity of conscious awareness.

Casting off the cloak of ignorance is not accomplished by reading or listening to words.

Though the mind is always active in the external world, it does not represent the real person. It is but an appearance. We need to ask, "Who is real?" "Who, before all ancestors, am I?" Constantly asking "Who am I?" encourages the mind to look to Mind, putting an end to human misery.

The above lines, paraphrased from the words of Ramana Maharshi, could be rewritten in a thousand ways. The sentences — not the words, but that which is meant — contain the essence of all wisdom. This truth may appear in any words, in any language. Finding it puts an end to seeking!

My friend Helen cautions, "David, watch the thinker. It is the illusion, the destroyer of joy." And indeed, not until my thoughts slowed down and came to a stop did I glimpse things as they *are*. Then I changed from the thinker to the knower who is one with deity.

After all the words are said and written, the hydrangeas still bloom and the pansies crowd and jostle each other to reach the light. The pine tree rocks gently in the wind, dropping a cone. The little brown tohee follows it as it rolls and gobbles up the pine seeds sprung from the cone.

Now I am no longer outside as a watcher. I am one with all. I am the pine tree, the cone, the seed, the bird, the crowding flowers.

CHAPTER FOUR

Love

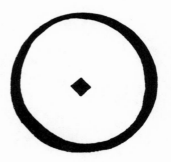

Love

Put away the sponge of knowledge
and listen to the song of love.

The man sitting at the table by a large window watches the white clouds after a rain as they pile up above the hilltops. Suddenly he see that what he views is not out there, but right where he is. It is consciousness itself. He is aware of a welling up of love without object or desire, a pure and all-encompassing love that blots out the illusion of the man sitting at a table.

To whom will this man speak of what he knows? He can tell no one. He holds the secret in his heart. Never again will familiar objects and experiences seem as solid as he once believed them to be.

Listen to your heart. Feel from your center and know the truth. It is always there. "Be still and know." Divine love is all around you.

※

Where is God's infinite love? Where can it be seen and recognized? It is within the perfect Self—the Self that I am and you are. What else is this but love itself? What else is there for you or I to be?

※

> Pursued, love vanishes;
> Held, love is not.
> To have love is to be it;
> To give love is love's lot.

※

When the heart opens wide to unobjectified, unpossessing love, it brings peace to others near and far.

※

The widest, deepest understanding of love is a concept, and thus, still a limited glimpse. No concept can come close to supreme knowing; no words can approach the wonder of the greatest galaxy of suns or the tiniest petal of the humblest weed.

Still, it's extraordinary that I know and feel love wrapping me around and through with its light.

※

The words, "God is love," are worthless unless love is experienced and lived.

Love is a wonder. As the grass, the tree, we, and thee, love *is*. It cannot be measured, weighed, counted, or examined under a microscope. Love is not a tangible thing that can be possessed by the me-person. It is like existence — a mystery unknowable except as experience.

※

Where is God's infinite love to be seen and recognized? Within the perfect Self — the Self I am and you are. *Pure Awareness*

※

The newest, smallest leaf lately sprung and the yellowed, fallen one are the same. The tender flower and the coated seed — these, too, are the same. They are one in love and as love.

※

For most love is an attachment to this or that image or sensation. Can I describe its true meaning? No, not any more than I can describe the principle called awareness or God.

I can, however, tell what it is not. It is not an image. Nor is it an object of desire. But I love, oh yes, I love! It's the fire of life. But what is that? The heart sings it. In stillness you can hear it — wordless song, soundless sound, ever awesome, ever amazing.

※

Everywhere conscious awareness tells of love. It is meat and drink. It is sleeping and waking and the simple things of life. It is ever present, all surrounding — closer than the beat of your heart.

The heart sings of unspeakable love. Its only wish is to share, to give—not alms—but truth, the greatest gift.

Listen to the song of your heart. Even though it has no words, you and I do the best we can to interpret. This world is full of magic. The impossible *is* ever possible. Amen.

CHAPTER FIVE

Suffering

Suffering

Come away from the bogs of remembrance *Past*
and fears in the shadowy cave.* *future*

Some people worry about wrecked buildings and mourn
the wrecked bodies littering the highways. They see
countries wrecked by war, cities wrecked by earth-
quakes. Most will never know that these sights are only
appearances to the limited sight of those of us separated
from our God.

As long as we are attached to material things and to our
idea of a beginning and an end, we continue to suffer. We
continue to live in fear of accidents, sickness, aging, and
death.

Life is not to blame for our blindness to truth. It's up to each of us to turn away from our conditioned thoughts and discover the wonder of life and awareness.

🌠

I read stuffy, pompous words about the human condition, the cruelty we impose on ourselves and the planet we inhabit. I weep about our apparent helplessness.

Who will save us from our ignorance and our superficial concerns? Are we waiting in vain for the liberator? Is it up to each of us to discover truth within ourselves?

Yes. For only through liberating ourselves first, can we begin to liberate others.

🌠

The unknowing ones call for peace at every street corner. Isn't this a search for peace outside the Self? Find serenity in the heart. Find the God Self that is consciousness—untouched by any superficial human limitation.

🌠

If we wish to see change for the better externally, we must first see change within ourselves. Peace begins in the heart.

🌠

The world and all its struggling, suffering, and battling is but a divine plan for our advancement to the spiritual splendor of a new day.

We accept the shadowy places, knowing that the shadows could not exist without light. Light is the cause. The shadows are but an effect of the light.

What we ordinarily look on as the external world is only an image of reality based on our limited sight. The tragedy is that we see this world as duality — ourselves and the world out there. We don't see what is nearest, most loving, and most powerful.

From this blindness comes all our misery. God is our only *real* world. It is here that we find love and peace beyond understanding.

How can we know perfection without the contradistinction of a so-called hell? Isn't it pain that causes us to yearn for heaven? Isn't the Resurrection the contradistinction of the Crucifixion?

Any indication of darkness in life is rooted in mistakenly identifying with a dual world. We are all trapped there until we discover the truth that our existence is synchronous.

Peace is never external. It is the awareness we are. It never needs changing or improving. Awareness or consciousness is ever perfect.

Do not worry about the empty places. We are all prone to them. They only *seem* empty.

What can I say about all that I have burdened my mind with? The beliefs in duality, the misery, and the brief pleasures had a purpose. The anguish, the joy, the good, and the bad all brought me to where I am today. I give thanks for every depressing day of it!

CHAPTER SIX

Consciousness

Consciousness

Out of the darkness
of memory-burdened mind
rises a star, enlightening
the wonder of consciousness itself.

Seeing the immensity of life, I am emptied of all personal concerns. I am awed by the mystery that surrounds us — consciousness as body, tree, grass, and grain of sand. It leaves the mind floundering like a fish out of water.

The life awareness I am is lighter than a snowflake, clearer than a mountain stream. Hardly a day passes that I don't see a reflection of this pure light in the eye of another I pass on the street.

There is so much more to conscious existence than newspapers, magazines, and television would have us believe.

Appearances are not truth. The images on the television screen are not the principle of television. They merely represent its functioning. The moving picture is not the screen.

Similarly, appearances of birth, change, and death are based on our judgments about time. In reality, neither time nor space are as most of us believe them to be.

There is a light that illumines the heart and has no source and no end. This light is the eternal *I*, free of desire, contention, jealousy, pros and cons, likes and dislikes. It is also free of emotions and any sense of ego.

This light casts a new meaning over all. It is happiness without cause or condition. It reveals the wonder of conscious being. It is a light of praise and thanksgiving for the light itself, which is love unbound, love beyond object or want.

In most of us, the light is hidden so deeply we cannot see its gleam nor hear its song. But everywhere, in every land, some have broken through the barriers and revealed the light. Organized religions and political systems fear the light. They worry it might destroy our institutions. Bearers of the light are often persecuted, hounded, imprisoned, even slain under legal pretexts. But *nothing* can destroy the light. It is as unextinguishable as the pure and eternal I.

Light has no age. It is always new. We are light. Everything is light. We are forever new. Everything *is*.

Consciousness cannot be changed or altered. Consciousness *is*! It is omnipresent, omnipotent, and omniscient. What can we do but *be* it, know the joy and light of it here and now in the present and eternal moment, love wholly and in freedom, never know death, never be lonely but be in the glorious presence of infinite being?

God's consciousness is ever present and equally powerful everywhere. It is here to be seen and recognized, not as an image, but as that from which the image comes.

The infinity of the universe is here and now in our awareness. Every moment, the knowing, illumined one is unattached and free.

All that exists *is* consciousness. My world is thus conscious awareness. In fact, my world is not mine at all, but God's.

I, the Self, am neither born nor dying.
I am free of space and time.
Before the Adam myth, I, awareness am.
I am all things visible and invisible,
The galaxies, the atom, the insignificant rose.
In secret stillness I am known.
I, as awareness, am the world I see.

Consciousness, which doesn't age, is eternal. Consciousness is really all you are.

There is nothing going on in the universe but God's action, God's being, all of which is here, in this moment.

CHAPTER SEVEN

Reflections

Reflections

Life is not mine.
Now love I more
and know the wonder
of God living me.

Ageless One

As I walk along the street, I pass three men bending over a car engine. Other people wheel baskets with dirty clothes to the nearby laundry. Many speed by in cars or on bicycles. An ancient woman bent low moves slowly with the help of a cane. Two runners in jogging clothes divide and pass the old one as if she were a tree stump obstructing the way. Only the old woman leaning on her cane smiles at me. Is she the only one who sees we are not separate? Is this ancient one full of pain the only one who has glimpsed beyond the limits of habit-thinking that close the eyes?

How do I know the old crone with the witch-like visage is different from the rest? What do I see? I see that wizened face full of light, shining with a joy that belies the appearance of old age and arthritic bones. Hers is the light of an ageless one who knows no pros and cons, nor ends and beginnings. I salute her. She laughs and holds out a bit of blue filagree she has plucked from the grass. I walk on feeling lifted up.

Conditioning

We are conditioned by patterns of thinking passed down from one generation to another. Indeed, we are like computers, programmed for one set of ideas, actions, and reactions considered the norm. Anything outside that programming is suspect, doomed to be discarded as unintelligible and unwanted.

Where is the law that says all things are not possible? No such law exists. Everything is possible to one who understands that limits created by humans can be dispensed with.

As long as we honor a way simply because it is established, we dishonor the infinite possibilities around us. If the ape had refused to stand and walk because apes had not done so before, where would the human being be now?

By seeing that no limits exist, we allow miracles to occur.

She asked him, "Why, when you're out walking, do you usually walk with your mouth open?"

The old one laughed. "It must be because I walk in constant wonder, every step in awe of the pavement I walk on, the warmth of the sun on my face, the woman in blue driving the van, in awe of you, your bright questioning eyes, of each breath I take, of the pulse of the heart. All of it's so utterly wonderful—especially the awareness in which everything lives, moves, and has being."

"I wish I could see it that way."

"But how can you not? It's the fact of existence. Everything tells it. The roses and yellow oxalis blooms tell it, even as the insects feed on them. Don't you see?"

"All I see are the ordinary things of every day. Oh, I want to see the wonder of it. I believe you when you tell me you see it. But I have to be true to myself."

"But are you being true? Are you sure what you call 'true' isn't an agreement to go along with your conditioned beliefs? Go back before that conditioning began, before your mind became set. Go back to the free, open state of your birth."

"Wait! I have a glimpse of the wonder you speak of. If I could just get at it!"

"Stop trying. Leave your wishes out of it. You *are* that pure little one. That child within never left you, though for a while you hid it from yourself by your belief in what you call 'ordinary.' Put that ordinary belief aside and let the new awareness *be.* You are the child of wonder, of unadulterated awareness. Now I see a new light in your eyes! Tears? Let them come. It's natural to feel the joy of reunion."

Judgments

I never dreamed how much of the day was spent in criticizing my food, my clothes, my hair, my face, or in complaining about the weeds in the garden, the images on the television screen, and so on, endlessly.

The wearisome burden of daily judgments, when recognized, becomes a load one gratefully sets aside. What a relief it is to be finished with the me-sense. This discovery alone results in a feeling of youth, a revelation of new-found energy, time, and freedom.

The bulk of our problems arises from judgments of ourselves, our peers, and our world.

Until now, I had never seen my world. It is new and filled with countless nuances of form, color, and sound which before were blotted out by my judgments. Now the veil is lifted and I have discovered awareness filled with wonders! I see now that God is the only real consciousness and that I am not separate. Now I begin to truly enjoy my Self.

Until you've tried living without commenting on every little thing all day, you can't know what a joyful revelation it is to perceive without judging.

We judge all things good and evil. But beyond human thought there is good in everything and purpose in all the joys and tragedies of human existence.

Separation

The separation of any facet of life from the whole is where all our problems originate.

We struggle to conquer nature. How ridiculous! We really struggle against ourselves, our universe, and all that is ours. We *are* nature. We are not separate. We are here now as consciousness.

Should we be amazed that all is one? Why do we think of ourselves as apart from birds and animals, believing that we are alone in our silent contemplation?

It is one thing to preach oneness, but if it isn't fully understood and lived, what is preached becomes an empty gesture.

To honor flesh as apart from rock, tree, and water makes no sense. Just as every growing form of life is related, so too are all structures. Because of this interdependence, we cannot afford to despise anything.

The feeling of separation is a common illusion. We can only dispel it by *knowing* truth.

When we presume that we are separate from trees, flowers, or this planet, we presume the impossible. We have no life outside God's consciousness. Our need is to surrender all sense of ego and know that it is God that lives as us and as everything.

Death

I am as free as the grass, the daisy, and the blue sky. Grass may be cut and eaten by cattle, but it grows back again. And so do I. I am life unslayable. I am the consciousness which sits and smiles. I am ineffable awareness.

Nothing dies or disappears. Everything is present as it always has been. Because life may move in a direction where the eyes cannot see, there is no reason to believe anything is gone. Nothing is gone. Everything is here. There is no other place to be.

All that dies is the carcass — the unreal concept. The real body of light — consciousness eternal — does not die.

How rewarding it is when I can face my image in the mirror and think, "I am not the aging person I see. I am not limited by time or breath. I am not this image. I am liberated and unbound. I am THAT."

All that I am is consciousness. By surrendering the limited I or ego and its supposed possessions, I pass through the first death unscathed. The second death then means no more to me than what a caterpillar experiences when it sheds its old skin and emerges into the full light of a new day as a butterfly.

Some ask, "When I die doesn't consciousness die, too?" Our concept of the body dies, but consciousness is eternal and unchanging.

The sooner we rid ourselves of the hypothetical limitations of the body, the sooner we discover our real state of being — serenity. Only the illusion dies. Reality is eternal.

We are in the habit of thinking that matter is dead. But in reality nothing is dead. Life is wondrous, for it includes every substance without division.

We are all related. Everything is energy, appearing as molecules and atoms — light in bondage.

 God

I discovered that there is no god up there in the sky, no god on a cross, no god in Canterbury, Rome, or Mecca. God is in this place where I am, in the perfect presence of awareness, the I, I am. Here is God, here and now as the consciousness I am. And this is true whether I am in Canterbury, Rome, Mecca, California, or on the moon.

Though it thinks about the infinite, the human brain does not know infinity. Like God, it is beyond conception.

Helen's Letter

Dear David,

Even though we may believe it to be so, there is never any dimming of awareness. Awareness, the principle that is consciousness, eternally *is*. You may walk through marble halls and eat from plates of gold, but this does not affect the way you live. It is foolish to feel you must live in either a poor dwelling or a ruggedly simple house. If you allow anything to move you off course, you become victim to the illusion that light can be dimmed.

Always stay at the center of perfect balance. In other words, keep your attention firmly fixed on the constant omnipresence of God. You will then be at home in a palace or a hovel and your place of worship will always be with you and will not depend on any visible representation.

As often as your life allows it, retreat to the closet of your heart and seek to know the eternal presence in which we all live. Keep the eye single: Fix the attention on eternal qualities, rather than on transitory appearances and you will understand that all mortal fears are nothing.

If I could tell you more, dear friend, I would, but only you can discover the astonishing marvel that is all life as well as you. No one can do this for you.

Helen Freeman Corle

Stillness

Every moment is new. Yet I continue to pollute the new-ness with habitual thinking, imaging, and remembering. Thus, I probably have never seen the true newness of each moment unless I have practiced being still.

In stillness I am no longer the limited me. Free as pure awareness, I am where symbols and words do not exist.

I used to think of meditation as sitting upright for endless empty hours. Now I find I can attain that same still mind doing daily chores or even talking on the phone. I find myself aware of energy, beauty, and joy in being.

Put the busy thinker to bed and be still.

All things sought after are given to me when I clear my mind and keep it pristine through listening in deep still-ness. "If therefore thine eye be single, thy whole body shall be full of light."

Through stillness, I die to the world of duality and judg-ment. Through this absence of the me-person, the won-der of *I* is revealed. Here, the old divisions disappear along with the conditioned person. We are decondi-tioned and return to being unadulterated children. Only through the purity that is the child living within us can we behold life as it really is. Find that hidden child and be it!

I wonder if the two most beautiful words in language are not "Be still"? I have found wordless wonders when the mind is open and still. This experience of stillness reveals we *are* wonders.

Expectation

Expectation is rooted in time. It is a concept, and as a concept, has no real substance — except for that which we give it.

If I stop waiting for something good to happen, I am never disappointed. On the contrary, I see what is and I find the wonder you and I are to be far more than anything I expected.

Responsibility

> I am the way I choose.
> I blame no one nor anything
> For problems I seem to suffer.
> I made them as they appear.
> And yet, no trap that's built
> Can hold the wondrous I, I am.
> As I live the truth I am,
> Love transforms the world I see.

Questions

Walking on two hind legs is no longer enough of a miracle. The present state of the human race is in a doldrum, a backwater. Remaining in it invites extinction. May we awaken and ask "Why?" before it's too late!

We yearn to know the power that makes up life, that grows a giant oak or hemlock from an acorn or a cone seed, and forms a rose, a leaf, a child. And what of the power that beats the heart and fashions all the infinite forms in which that power functions? What is this power and from where does it come?

I pass a mother who waits tapping her foot while her little one crouches in fascination over a wooly caterpillar. The mother calls, "Come child, you'll never learn to be a successful man squatting there in the dirt." Without looking up, the child asks, "Why?"

Think about that "Why?" Why do measurements of time, space, and numbers supposedly lead to success? Why is the life that causes the caterpillar to run for a tree of no importance? Why is the wonder of that consciousness that is child and caterpillar not important? Why are we bound to patterns of thinking that are supposed to make us useful citizens in society?

Listen to the child's question and ask yourself, "Why?" Continue asking "Why?" and you will begin to see endless wonders before you.

It's Later Than We Think

Though the great experiment called the human race is nearly over, it is not too late to understand. Scientists have seen through matter to the atom. They have discovered the invisible power that looks like nothing but is everything. Still, it hasn't dawned on them that the unnameable power that they have reached is what for centuries people have called God — the source of all power, matter, and life. It is beyond us to see, hear, or feel God. Yet this presence is all around us *as us*.

The understanding and living of this reality can stay the vanishing. Come, it's later than we think!

Suggested Reading

Goldsmith, Joel S. *The Infinite Way*. DeVorss & Company, P.O. Box 550, Marina del Rey, California 90294. 1984.

First published in 1947, this book delineates the basic spiritual teachings of the Goldsmith philosophy.

Goldsmith, Joel S. *A Parenthesis in Eternity*. Harper & Row, 10 East 53rd Street, New York, New York 10022. 1986.

Joel Goldsmith's most current work, it provides a comprehensive look at living the mystical life within a context of realizing higher consciousness.

Maharshi, Ramana.* *Talks with Ramana Maharshi*. Ramana Publications, P.O. Box 77, Victor, New York 14564. 1984.

This is the most complete record available of the transcribed

---

*Not to be confused with Maharishi Mahesh Yogi, well-known advocate of Transcendental Meditation.

words of the Hindu sage. It includes a thorough exposition of his philosophy of Self-inquiry based on a pursuit of knowledge of the Self through asking the question, "Who am I?"

Maharshi, Ramana. *Spiritual Teaching of Ramana Maharshi*. Shambala Publications, 314 Dartmouth Street, Boston, Massachusetts 02117. 1972.

An overview of Ramana Maharshi's philosophy in question-and-answer form, with an introduction by Carl Jung.

Maharshi, Ramana. *Be As You Are: The Teaching of Sri Ramana Maharshi*. Edited by David Godman. Arkana Paperbacks, (Routledge & Kegan Paul, Ltd.), 9 Park Street, Boston, Massachusetts 02108. 1985.

Provides a record of the spiritual teacher's conversations with students at his ashram in India. Chapter introductions by editor Godman offer explanatory material for readers unfamiliar with Maharshi's teachings.

Samuel, William. *Awareness & Tanquillity*. Mountain Brook Publications, P.O. Box 7474, Mountain Brook, Alabama 35253. 1967.

An examination, based on the author's experience, of how surrender of the personality and ego lead to an understanding of the perfection that already resides within.

Samuel, William. *The Child Within Us Lives!* Mountain Brook Publications, P.O. Box 7474, Mountain Brook, Alabama 35253. 1986.

An expansive work that examines how discovery of the inner Self or Child leads to awakening. Ties metaphysics, religion, and science together, showing how the contemplative philosophies of the East can be actively and pragmatically lived in a Western culture.

About the author

David Manners was born in 1900 in Halifax, Nova Scotia. In his earlier days he wrote jacket copy for a New York publisher, sold paintings and sculpture in a Manhattan art gallery, and went on to act in the theater and on film. Later in his career, he ran a guest ranch in California's Mojave Desert where he first began to deeply consider the question, "Who Am I?" His spiritual experiences led to major changes in his life and to selling the ranch and moving to Pacific Palisades.

In recent years, Manners began recording his thoughts in a journal. He contributes to various spiritual publications including the *Science of Thought Review*, and is author of *Look Through (An Evidence of Self Discovery)*. He now lives in Santa Barbara where he shares his experiences in consciousness with others on a similar path.

Cover and text design by John Bailey

Typeset in Bembo by Stanton Publication Services

Cover painting by Stanton MacDonald-Wright
Abstraction on Spectrum (Organization, 5) 1914
Des Moines Art Center; Coffin Fine Arts Trust Fund

Printed on acid-free paper by Braun-Brumfield